Introduction
   A Teacher ... y
   Kids with

Chapter One

What is Dysgraphia in a Child
   Different impacts of dysgraphia
   What causes dysgraphia?
Dysgraphia versus dyslexia

Chapter Two
   How to Find Out if Your Child Has Dysgraphia
   Causes of Dysgraphia

Chapter Three
   Symptoms of Dysgraphia in a Child

Chapter Four
   How to Treat the Symptoms of Dysgraphia in Kids Immediately
   Academic Interventions for Dysgraphia
   At-Home Interventions for Dysgraphia

Chapter Five
   Teaching Children with Dysgraphia
      Remedial Strategies
      Compensatory Strategies
      Creativity note

Chapter Six
   Treating Dysgraphia with Therapy
   How is dysgraphia analysed?

What medications are accessible?

Chapter Seven

What to Do If Your Child Has Dysgraphia

Treatment

Chapter Eight

Living with dysgraphia for Kids

Chapter Nine

Fun Activities to Correct Dysgraphia in Children

Introduction

A Teacher's Note: How I Teach Handwriting to my Kids with Dysgraphia

I may have wondered and thought that things were not right when my 6-year old had difficulty for some weeks to derive at the 3 letter word that his name has.

However, as regards a lot of firstborn children, who do not have brothers and sisters to compare to, I have no idea of what to get. I forced him severally to write. I have no idea that dysgraphia was the problem. Many individuals with dysgraphia, for different purposes, usually have difficulty transmitting what the ears hear or what the eyes see and also delivering the information to form words and letters.

Apart from handwriting which Dysgraphia affects, it also affects a whole lot more:

Effects of Dysgraphia:

- It affects Spelling

- It affects composition

- It affects punctuation and grammar and

- It also affects drawing as well as coloring in young people.

The difficulty that pertains to Dysgraphia also affects different skill problems like:

- Visual-spatial weaknesses

- Poor motor processing skills and

- Poor fine motor skills

How I Teach Handwriting to mu Kids with Dysgraphia

A lot of years have gone by since pushing that 6-year old to write his 3 letter name, and I hope to have the feeling that I have been educated with a couple of things. I have discovered the most efficient way to educate kids with dysgraphia to write, to begin with, some modifications.

Start With Modifications

I adjust and change how much and the type of writing my kids usually do. When it comes to a traditional school, kids of about 5 or 6 years of age are meant to write for a long period all through the day.

Handwriting is a major thing going on in almost all classrooms. It assists a teacher in being up to date

with the movements and home works.

Close to the beginning of learning, the handwriting was done at the time of handwriting instruction.

While it was going on, I begin with a salt tray. Then I go-ahead to form a multi-sensory writing surface by discharging either an inch or two of salt into a little depth pan. While I checked through my early learners' letter sounds, I ensure they draw as many letters as they possibly can without not having to submerge into the salt. Errors are canceled out, and the multi-sensory component assists the memory.

 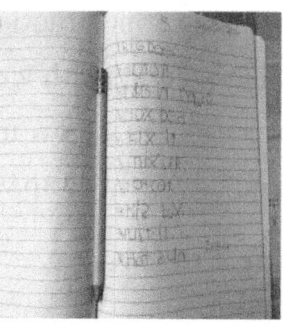

When you have come to know some things here, I transfer my knowledge to a small dry erase board, likely the ones that do not have lines. There the one with lines on one of the sides, and the other side is blank. Purchase a few odorless dry erase pens in colors that children like and make your child write down a couple of letters. At the initial point, while checking out, I will say a sound, and my child will have to write down the letter I say next. Note: I check out letter sounds for a long time so that my kids who have dyslexia will have an idea of them.

The next item we will discuss is about fat pencils and composition books. While spelling is going on, I spell out about 5-10 words or phrases for my child to write down in his book. Give your child the freedom to select the size of the letter he is free with for his hand.

It is not every dysgraphia kid who likes to write large letters. During this situation, my kid's handwriting is majorly covered up with writings that have both upper and lower case. It is now my aim to make their hands strong and cover them up with handwriting.

Teaching Cursive

At the time when I am convinced that my child is quite alright with writing his spelling words to his composition book, I change to cursive instruction. However, the most efficient program I know of is from the Logic of English, and it is known as The Rhythm of Handwriting.

Note that the program is full of multi-sensory, starting with the kinds of strokes that have each letter. When writing is being done, the verbal cues that the stroke is made use of will be called out.

Remediation for Dysgraphia

A few of you have not been all that happy as you read through the modifications that I use for my dysgraphia kids. Before you begin to have the fear that our instruction is not good enough, while we taught about the beginning stages of handwriting, we have our attention on remediation.

Remediation is making the foundation of our skills to be strong enough. Meanwhile, while we talk about dyslexia, it will focus on checking out and lecture with an Orton Gillingham based reading program.

For dysgraphia, this makes for improving:

- Enhancing visual-spatial awareness
- Motor skills: large and gross muscle as well as fine motor skills and
- Motor processing skills

Remediation is the major focus of assisting kids with dysgraphia from kindergarten through to middle school. Since dysgraphia can get affected by the likes of visual-spatial skills, processing speeds, and motor skills, there are still some different ways for remediating dysgraphia. If you are in search of methods to remediate your kids with dysgraphia, you should take my Parent Class: Teaching Handwriting to Kids With Dysgraphia.

You should know that the class will look at an in-depth look at:

- How it affects learning
- What dysgraphia is
- How to modify instruction for kids with dysgraphia
- Ways to make visual perception better
- How to teach kids to organize their writing
- How to strengthen working memory
- How to strengthen fine motor skills
- Ways to strengthen gross motor skills as well as motor planning skills
- An extensive list of resources for teaching kids with dysgraphia
- How to implement the best accommodations for kids that have dysgraphia

Accommodations for Dysgraphia

The last stages of my handwriting instruction bring about appropriate accommodations into my kids' learning. Note that accommodations are procedures and ways that permits kids to complete assignments at their grade level at their thinking ability.

For dysgraphia, this may be:

• Making use of some form of speech-to-text program

• Permitting the student to choose cursive or print

• Permitting the use of spell checkers

• Making use of graph paper for organizing written work

• Permitting school work to be typed

• Dictating written work to a scribe(either siblings or your parents)

• While in class, permit the student to have a designated note-taker

Accommodations are a major part of assisting kids to be an independent learners. While my kids have more and more fluent with their writing and reading, I change them into some kind and all needed accommodations so that they can keep up with their studies and also preserve a level of staying on their own in keeping with their level of maturity as well as their age.

What You Need to Know About Dysgraphia

Dysgraphia does not show a lack of intelligence. Just as dyslexia, dysgraphia is also not outgrown and is different in how severe they are. All children are special, and all kids' modifications, accommodations, and remediations will not be the same. As an individual, you are sure of your child's ability. Your instruction aims to be sure that your kids are reliable and efficient writers, and they can express their writings well.

Chapter One

What is Dysgraphia in a Child

Dysgraphia is a learning incapacity described by issues with writing. It's a neurological issue that can influence kids or grown-ups. Notwithstanding writing words that are hard to peruse, Children with dysgraphia will in general utilize an inappropriate word for what they're attempting to impart.

The reason for dysgraphia isn't constantly known, however in grown-ups it some of the time pursues an awful accident.

When the condition is analyzed, you can learn procedures to help beat a portion of the difficulties it exhibits in school and throughout everyday life.

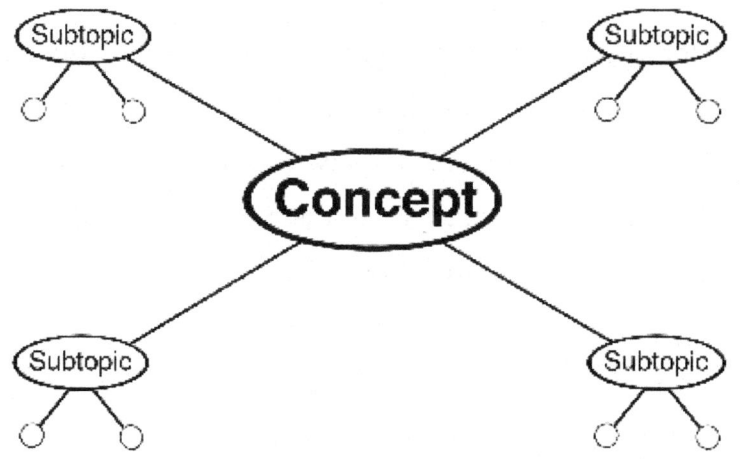

The Concept of Dysgraphia

Different impacts of dysgraphia

Children with dysgraphia regularly experience difficulty focusing on different things while writing. This can make it hard to take notes during class or a gathering in light of the fact that so much consideration is being paid to getting each word down on paper. Different things that are said might be missed.

Understudies with dysgraphia may likewise be blamed for being messy or apathetic on the grounds that their handwriting isn't slick. This can influence confidence and lead to nervousness, an absence of certainty, and negative frames of mind toward school.

Getting to Know You

1. My favorite time of day is: Wen I'm don with school
2. My favorite dinner is: Brokly cees soop (Broccoli cheese soup)
3. When I'm happy I usually show it by: Smyaling (smiling)
4. My favorite animal is: Waleshark (Whale shark)
5. If I could be an animal, I'd be a/an: Waleshark
6. If I have nothing to do on a Sunday afternoon, I usually: walkinserklds (Walk in circles)
7. I think it's important to be: Kined (Kind)
8. I think it's important to have: Spase for yor stuf
9. In my life, I hope that I get to: swim with a Walesarh
10. One very special person to me is: Dad
    Because: he poots food on the tadel (He puts food on the table)

Typical Handwriting of a child with Dysgraphia

What causes dysgraphia?

On the off chance that dysgraphia shows up in adolescence, it's normally the aftereffect of an issue with orthographic coding. This is a part of working memory that enables you to for all time recollect composed words, and the manner in which your hands or fingers must move to compose those words.

With dysgraphia, children or grown-ups make some harder memories arranging and executing the writing of sentences, words, and even individual letters. It isn't so much that you don't have a clue how to peruse, spell, or distinguish letters and words. Rather, your cerebrum has issues preparing words and writing.

At the point when dysgraphia creates in grown-ups, the reason is typically a stroke or other mind damage. Specifically, damage to the mind's left parietal projection may prompt dysgraphia. You have a privilege and left parietal flap in the upper piece of your mind. Each is related with a scope of aptitudes, for example, perusing and writing, just as tactile handling, including agony, warmth, and cold.

Dysgraphia versus dyslexia

Dyslexia is an understanding issue and dysgraphia is a writing issue, yet the conditions may once in a while be mistaken for each other. That is on the grounds that Children with dyslexia may likewise have issues with their writing and spelling.

It's conceivable to have both learning incapacities, yet it's essential to get an appropriate finding so you know whether one or the two conditions require consideration.

Chapter Two

How to Find Out if Your Child Has Dysgraphia

Dysgraphia is an impaired ability to learn to write or to present written expressions in a clear manner. It is a learning disability resulting from the nervous system deficiency in writing. In this situation, the fine motor abilities must have been deformed which leads to poor lettering productivity from the child. At an age when a child would already have been equipped with the necessary writing skills or expressions, an affected child would instead be found wanting and lagging in the graphical and coding area of learning.

A child with this learning deficiency should not however be regarded as unintelligent. That is, his inability to comprehend and to quickly understand the skill of writing does not define his entire learning skill. This is so because most of such children often perform extremely well with spoken expressions.

As growth takes place in the child, dysgraphia fades and this is because the child constantly manages to level up with the conventional writing techniques. However, there would still be evidences to commemorate that child's dysgraphia. Such would include poor hand positioning, disjointed and distorted production on symbols, etc.

If your child's pen-ability is poor, the chances are that the child is suffering from dysgraphia. Sitting back would be endangering his writing skills and you should consider being attentive to the child and then follow up with actions to correct the impairment.

Causes of Dysgraphia

Dysgraphia in a child can be brought about by several causes. It could develop on emotional grounds as well as physical grounds. For instance, a child who isn't attentive to his lettering will end victimizing himself to dysgraphia.

Moreover, there are other causes of dysgraphia in a child and they include:

- Language
- Dyslexia
- Memory

- Failure to Coordinate the Muscles
- Dyspraxia

Language

Difficulties in a language could cause a child impairment in writing. A child who is exposed to a multilingual environment will most definitely experience this problem. For instance, a child whose parents' converse in French is conversant with French. But in a school where subjects are taught in English, that child will develop a writing impairment for the English language. That is to say that the child is not much exposed to the structure of the language taught in school.

Dyslexia

This has to do with impairment in reading. A child with reading difficulties has problems in writing. Such child finds it difficult to encode graphic symbols to writing materials because of he lacks he sequential knowledge for the arrangement symbols in place.

Memory

When a child faces difficulties in remembering the structure of the language in use, putting the words in order becomes a problem. Such child may not even be aware of the proper sketching of each of the letters in that language and as such, it becomes difficult to write down an idea.

Dyspraxia

Perceptual problems could cause motor difficulties thereby making it difficult for the child to be aware or become conscious of during writing.

Chapter Three

Symptoms of Dysgraphia in a Child

To know whether or not a child is suffering from dysgraphia, writing materials must be made available. As a follow up, the child should be provided with series of writing tasks. It would then easy to tell, from how the child will respond, whether he/she has a writing impairment. Now, be attentive and do not be forced to censure severely at how the child would present the letters.

Moreover, a child could be suffering, instead, from dyslexia and dyspraxia which differ from dysgraphia. It is thus important to note and differentiate between these terms so as not to mix up things. Here are the things to look out for and that will help ascertain the dysgraphia condition of a child.

1. Distorted Lettering

This is very common in children with impaired writing ability. The letters do not stay synched and are always very poorly formed. Such a child tends to spend present the letters in a manner that appears so disorganized with almost a zero message passed in the expression.

2. Non-Linear Writing

On properly lined writing materials, the symbols would often drop from the lined margin to either the margin below or the margin above. There is difficulty in arranging the words on a straight line, whether vertically or horizontally. Even when it seems to the child as though the he is performing great in his symbols presentation, it is in truth very deformed.

3. Shaky Grip

The child's hand, especially the wrist will stay shaky while there is a pencil in his palm. This is certainly the primary cause of the distorted lettering produced by the child. While the hand remains shaky, there is loss of connection between the child's mind and his physical touch of the pen.

4. Poor Hand Positioning

Beginning from the elbow, the hand positioning does not promise a good lettering. And in the process, there is a feeling of discomfort which only but discourages the child from writing. Some children position their hand in a way that make it very impossible to produce a nicely written and readable expression. The child will also fail to paragraph well.

5. Pencil-Hard Gripping

In an attempt to make a good and presentable letters, a child becomes carried while handling the pencil. Observing his hand closely, you'll realize that a grip mark would appear on his fingers which is as a result of the hard grip of the pencil. Within a short period of writing, the grip begins to hurt and cause blood flow to come to a halt thereby causing the affected fingers to remain almost insensitive for a while.

6. Slow Writing

In a bid to attempt the construction of fine letters to form words and other expressions, there will be slowness in writing. If dictations are made, it will be difficult for the child to cope and while some children will completely halt writing, some others will have lots of omissions on the writing materials provided.

7. Poor Presentation of Ideas

With difficulties in writing and writing well, there will be the absence of coherence and cohesion in the presented idea. With fear for writing, the child will develop ineffective passages, whether he has been provided a guide book/booklet or not. These ideas will, of course, turn out to be somehow vague and mismatching even though the child knows the right thing to put down.

8. Phobia for Writing

The refusal to write or respond to instructions in a written form does not mean the child is unintelligent. There is the fear that he will not know what to do to perfect his writing skill since it had always been rough and unclear.

9. Tiredness After a Short Writing Period

As dictation or note copying progresses, the child becomes quickly tired and loses focus. Also, the tiredness is restricted to the pen or pencil in hand which when dropped, the depleted strength resurfaces. At such instance, the child loses out on vital points raised during the dictation or note copying.

10. Misuse of Capital and Small Letters

Somewhere in the middle of a write up, there will be a mix up in the placement of letter forms. The child will often consciously substitute capital letters for small. Also, he may have the intention of putting in a capital letter where necessary but his poorly formed handwriting denies him the liberty. This is the case in children who find it difficult to know what nouns require the use of capital letters even when they occur in the middle of a sentence.

Chapter Four

How to Treat the Symptoms of Dysgraphia in Kids Immediately

As an individual who has been diagnosed with dysgraphia or your kid, which is a problem in learning that has a big say in handwriting and fine motor skills, the next thing to do is to chase accommodations at home or in your place of work. While depending on the kind of dysgraphia you or your child may have, which ranges from the motor, dyslexic, or spatial, occupational therapy can be of assistance.

Note that you cannot cure dysgraphia, and the medications you will be prescribed to take will not be of help in any way. However, the issues of writing and fine motor skill can be corrected, most importantly, when you begin early to improve them. Comprehending teachers, parents and friends can be the major reason for rebuilding destroyed self-esteem as well as giving the much-needed support for adults and children who have dysgraphia.

Academic Interventions for Dysgraphia

The major thing the school of your child can perform to ensure that the symptoms of dysgraphia are controlled is to stop forcing the child to write or by taking other options such as speaking and typing. Few helpful alterations in the classroom may have:

Allow the student to take extra time on tests.

Children suffering from dysgraphia will take a longer time to form letters and words or fill the spaces provided. Giving the child extra time will make the child be stress-free and allow the children to have much more time to show you what they are capable of.

Provide worksheets.

Instead of needing children to copy down writings from the board into their note, which will put children that has dysgraphia on the bad side and receiving end, the teachers should endeavor to print out worksheets before the class commences and share them to the entire students for the benefit of all.

Remove neatness as a grading criterion.

Teachers giving low marks for handwriting not seen by them can be a problem for children suffering from dysgraphia and make the child feel inferior and that his effort was all for a waste. The teachers should make available word processing software if they fail to see a child's handwriting.

Reduce the length of written assignments.

While in science or math class sessions, the number of issues to be solved should be cut down.

Provide the student with the "teacher's copy" of the notes.

If this situation cannot work out, the teachers can permit another student to stand up and begin to distribute notes.

Allow students to substitute "keywords" for full sentences, anytime possible.

This is good because it removes all the time used in finding it difficult to write. However, you will still give the student a chance to reply to the questions with the right answers.

Create oral options for writing assignments.

This state that, permitting an oral version of full exams, or restoring a short worksheet with a fast oral lesson summary at the close of day.

Allow for some spelling errors.

If this is possible, the teachers should allow dictionaries to be used, especially when it comes to checking spellings to be sure.

Use physical accommodations.

Physical accommodations can include the likes of erasable pens, pencil grips as well as paper with raised lines, everything which assists students with dysgraphia work based on the skills of handwriting. Also, when it comes to Graph paper, which gives visual guidance for giving letters, space, and numbers is important. When large projects come into question, the Ghost line poster board is very efficient because it has a light grid.

Allow students to use computers with word processing software if it is possible. For another choice, the teachers should permit the students to make use of planning software prior to writing a long answer with the use of the hand.

At-Home Interventions for Dysgraphia

Around the beginning stages, you must work in tandem with your children's educational people to assist in improving their handwriting in their houses and also school. Below are the methods which you can take to complete it:

Teach typing.

The-teach typing is a sure life-saving method for every child that has been diagnosed with dysgraphia. Put your money in a recommended children typing program. You can invest for younger children, the Typing Instructor for Kids, and the classic Mavis Beacon Teaches Typing for teenagers. Give your child something whenever he or she practices on the computer, even if the child practices for as low as ten minutes every day.

Assist your child get a good grip on the pen or pencil.

In some circumstances whereby typing cannot take place, your child must hold her pencil or pen in the right way. Your child may not see the reason to alter the way she holds her pencil, but holding it the right way will reduce weakness in the hand which will make writing less painful and very smooth. A lot of pencil grips you can find around usually state that "tripod" grip should be what they should make use of. Meanwhile, the Grotto Grip Pencil Grasp Trainer has been produced and successfully tested by occupational therapists, and it is the most used grip for children.

Encourage your child to dictate sentences into a tape recorder before writing them on a paper.

This is good because his speaking skills will come out, and it gives the child the chance to put his attention on forming letters, without being confused in syntax and grammar.

Be a scribe for your child.

More children suffering from dysgraphia do not like the idea of attending to homework that has to do with handwriting, and this will lead to an easy homework taking too much time to finish. You can make your child crave writing by taking some pressure off your child when you decide and tell him you will write for him for a short time. For instance, when you want to write a paragraph, write down the first sentence while your child dictates while giving your child the chance to write the next sentence, continue with the same process till the assignment is completed. By so doing, the time in doing the homework will be short, and your child will not be stressed out and makes him crave for the next sentence.

Prompt your child to say the words as he writes them.

Saying what you write as a child makes some parts of the brain active, and it will make the child be focused and pay close attention.

Do letter-formation drills (print and cursive).

The letters do not have to be all that good. Meanwhile, the letters should be at least consistent and should be able to read through. Endeavor to make sure your child forms letters starting from the top rather than the bottom.

Use Handwriting Without Tears.

Hwtears.com is a program that has online tools and a workbook that is known to be efficient to people.

Engage in multi-sensory exercises.

Request your child to write in either the air, paint, or sand while making use of his finger. Through this way, the child will have a memory of the shape of the letter he wrote.

Keep letters inside the lines by writing on raised-line paper (therapyshoppe.com).

This kind of sensory-friendly paper will assist your children in having an idea of how far the lines are from each other which will make it easy to write on normal lined paper later on in their life.

Build muscle memory in fingers.

There is a learning specialist known as Kendra Wagner, he suggests this occupational therapy solution: "Have your child walk her index, middle finger up and down a chopstick, thumb, put it on a flat surface, as quickly as they can. Just the three 'grip' fingers should have contact with the chopstick.

Chapter Five

Teaching Children with Dysgraphia

A technique that is very familiar is to have the learners or students write basic information to reinforce the material. For instance, programs that deal with spellings usually encourage learners or students to write every spelling word 5 times or at most, 20 times. For some students, the kinesthetic process of putting down reinforces what is to be learned.

Nevertheless, for a tiny group of students or learners, instead of reinforcing or consolidating information, the steps of writing actually interfere with acquiring knowledge. These set of students find it difficult to write and consequently spend a lot of time, unlike their peers on a writing assignment.

Even at that, they remember less, that is, the act of writing greatly interferes with learning. Cognitively, much of their energy is spent on the steps that they usually do not learn or at times even process the content of what they are practicing.

A few of these students with serious dysgraphia may complete a writing assignment and later have to go through it again to determine what they have put down, particularly in a copying task or assuming that they are concentrating on neatness.

It is expected by educators that students learn from the process of writing, still these students find that the process of writing interferes with learning. How, then, can they learn to make use of the process of writing to express their ideas?

Why does this happen?

Dysgraphia is an issue with the writing process. For these learners or students, there is a deep reason that their papers are bad or that their speed is either too slow or too fast. It is not fair to label them as poorly motivated, lazy, impulsive, or careless. As these interpretations may have some truths on the surface, they are not the root of what is occurring.

The root for dysgraphia is discovered within the processing system involved with sequencing, particularly the motor movements which should not only be automatic, but sequential.

Dysgraphia in students need to work on both the remediation and compensations strategies. Compensations are technique to bypass the issue and lower the bad impact on learning, though it is accomplished by avoiding the difficulty, which is, changing the assignment expectations, or making use of strategies to help a particular aspect of the task. In addition, compensations can be termed 'bypass' strategies or accommodations, the latter term used frequently in legal situations.

On the other hand, remediation offers extra structured practice or re-teaching of the skill or concept making use of specialized techniques to match the student's processing style and need. A parent or astute teacher must determine the point at which the student becomes perplexed or starts to find it difficult. Does it start immediately the student begins to write? Is it halfway through the paragraph? Is it when the student attempts to imagine more complicated ideas instead of just write a sentence or work on copying a task? When these determinations are made, it is key to know which component of the task because the confusions or struggles. Is it because of the manuscript or cursive? Is it the steps of coping with mechanics as you write? Is it the steps of attempting to imagine and plan as you write?

Remedial Strategies

It is extremely important that students do not fully avoid the process of writing, no matter how serious their dysgraphia. Writing is a critical life skill necessary for filling out forms, writing checks, signing documents, taking telephone messages or writing a grocery list. So, students should write, even if they can't maintain writing for longer periods.

Students who are much younger should receive remediation in automaticity, letter form, and fluency. They need specific multisensory techniques that will encourage them to verbalize the motor sequences of the form of letters (for instance, b is big stick down, circle away from my body). Furthermore, students should make use of large air writing to grow a more efficient motor memory for the sequence of processes necessary in making every letter.

This is due to air writing which leads students to make use of many more muscles than they use when writing with a pencil. Multisensory techniques should be utilized for impacting knowledge on both cursive and manuscript writing. The techniques need to be worked on regularly so that the letters are fairly automatic before the student is questioned to make use of these skills to communicate ideas.

A few students may be able to not only copy, but write single sentences with a fair degree of ease, but they find it tough with paragraph writing. These types of students will need to be enlightened on techniques that will make them to perform every subpart prior to pulling together all the parts. Substantial modelling will also be important at every stage for the student to experience success. For instance, when writing paragraph students can be enlightened with these following steps listed below;

- Think deep about your ideas and expand on every part of the ideas

- Put together the ideas you want to express.

This kind of organization is simply performed with the use of visual graphic organizers. For instance, you can design a mind map so that the main idea is located in a circle in the center of the page and assisting facts are written on lines coming out of the main circle, familiar to the spokes on a wheel or arms of a spider. A variety of visual organizer formats can be used, with separate formats appropriate for distinctive situations.

- **Analyze your graphic organizer to determine assuming that you added all of your ideas.**

Assuming that you have issues or critical words you may want to add in your writing. Having this reference list will support your writing flow more because you wouldn't have to stop to imagine of how to write the big words.

- **Write a draft of your paragraph, concentrating on the ideas or content.**

Assuming that you have a personal computer, it is ideal if you type your draft directly on the keyboard.

This will enable it much simpler to revise and proofread.

- **Proof and editing;**

It is required of you to make use of specific techniques and strategies to proofread your paper, checking for appropriate use of capitalization, grammar, and punctuation. Then make use of a spell checker to fix your spelling.

- Go through on your paragraph, incorporating the corrections you determined earlier.

- Proofread your paragraph again, revising and editing them

- Grow a final product, either in written form or typed.

A simple way to remember these processes is to imagine of the word POWER

P- Plan your paper

O- Organize your thoughts and ideas

W- Write your draft

E-edit your work

R-revise your work, producing a final draft

A few dysgraphic students have big issues with spelling, particularly if sequencing is a big problem for them. In addition, various dysgraphic students witness dyslexia, a sequential processing issue that impacts reading and spelling. These students need very specific remedial support in learning how to spell phonetically.

It is important that they are capable to lead unknown words making use of phonetic equivalences. Assuming that they are able to spell logically and also phonetically, they will be able to make use of a phonetically-based spell checker, like a spell checker among the Franklin resource products. These handheld devices know words using phonetic logic instead of relying on the orthographic sequence, as to do most spell checkers on a computer word processing program.

Below, presents a poem which exemplifies the reason a computer spell checker may not be sufficient for a few students with spelling difficulties.

A small poem with regards to computer spells checkers

'Eye halve a spelling chequer it came with my pea sea it plainly marques our my revue Miss steaks eye kin knot sea'

'Eye strike a key and type a word and weight four it two say weather eye am wrong oar write it shows me strait weigh'.

'As soon as a mist ache is maid it nose bee fore too long And eye can put the error rite its rare lea ever wrong'.

'Eye have run this poem threw it I am shore your pleased two no its letter perfect awl the weigh My checker toiled me sew'.

Another important aspect of remedial support that is particularly critical for young kids, involves the student's pencil grip. Students should be supported and encouraged to make use of a regular and efficient pencil grip right from the start of their writing experience. The distance from the learner or student's finger to the pencil point should be regularly be between ¾-1.

Pressure on the pencil should not be too heavy or too light, rather it should be moderate. The angle of the pencil should exactly be on 45 percent with the page and slanted toward the student's writing arm.

The long edge of both the paper and the writing arm of the student should be parallel, such as railroad tracks. Pencil habits with some young students can be changed to a more appropriate form by making use of a plastic pencil grip (many of which are available in the market in numerous shapes and formats), it is more simpler and efficient to say some encouragement words on students at the very start of their writing experience to grow these appropriate habits through frequent modelling and positive feedback.

Much older students who have grown firm habits, even if the habits are yet to be efficient, see that it's very time consuming to make changes. So, when making a choice on adapting a student's habits, it is extremely critical to consider the time and energy ratio. The amount of time is worthy to be necessary to make changes to assist the student to be more efficient. If not, it is important to ensure the student has automatic and efficient compensatory strategies.

Various students with dysgraphia are very slow in their writing performances. If it is the case, it is important to determine what led to the slowness. Is it the organization of ideas? Or the formulation of ideas? If so, it is required that more work needs to be done on pre-organization strategies and this student's language formulation skills needs to be assessed by a language and speech pathologist.

Is the slowness in actually making the letters the cause of the student's slowness? If it is the case, the student needs remedial practice in forming letters independently, without imagining about the content. It can be done using multisensory techniques, which includes saying the letter or the sequence of movements as you write the letter, using large air writing techniques, that is, writing the letter in the air using two fingers, with wrist and elbow fairly straight, although flexible.

Various students find it difficult with writing and become eagerly fatigued with the process of writing due to their inefficient pencil grip and bad motor sequencing. In many situations, an occupational therapist, particularly one using a sensory integration philosophy, can assist in the remedial process.

Also, there are temporary remedial techniques a teacher or parent can make use of a warm-up or as a writing break. A few suggestions for helping reduce stress and calming the writing hand follow. Students can perform any of these for ten seconds before writing or when they have started writing.

- Do not shake hands violently, but fast

- Rub hands together and concentrate on the feeling of warmth

- If on clothing with some mild texture, rub hands on thighs, close to knees

- Use the thumb of the dominant hand to click the top of a ballpoint pen as you hold it in that hand. Do it again with the index finger

- Work on sitting pushups by placing every palm on the chair with fingers facing forward.

Compensatory Strategies

The whole objective of compensations is to assist the student perform more automatically and yet participate in and gain from the writing task. The objective is to let the student to go around the issue so that he or she can then concentrate more fully on the content. Some instances (strategies) include:

- Understanding: comprehend the student's performance variabilities and inconsistencies

- Cursive or Print: let the student to use either form. Various dysgraphic students are comfortable with manuscript printing. Assuming getting started is a issue, encourage pre-organization strategies, like using graphic organizers.

- Note taking: offer student with copy of full notes to fill in missing parts of his own notes. Also, offer a partially full outline so the student can fill in the details under many headings. As a variety, offer the details and student will fill in headings as they pay attention. Furthermore, let student to tape record critical assignments and take oral examinations.

- Computer: encourage students to feel comfortable using a word processor on a computer. Students can be enlightened in their first grade to type sentences directly on the keyboard. Doing that will not totally remove handwriting for the kid, because handwriting is still very important but computer skills will be invaluable for bigger tasks.

For older students, encourage use of a speech recognition program joined with the word processor so the student can read his papers instead of typing them. This increases efficiency and speed and lets the student to concentrate more fully on complicated thoughts and ideas.

• Encourage regular use of spell checker to reduce the total demands of the writing task and encourage students to wait until the end to be concerned about spelling.

• Encourage the use of an electronic resource like a spell check component in a Franklin Language Master to further reduce the demands. Assuming that student has reoccurring reading issues, a Language Master with a speaking component can support because it will read or say the words.

• Have student proofread papers after delaying them. Assuming that students proofread as soon as they write, they may read what they intended instead of what was actually written.

• Don't count off for poor spelling in class assignments, on first drafts, or on examination. Nonetheless, depending on age, student probably is held responsible for spelling in final drafts completed at home.

- Staging; students complete assignments in logical process or increments rather than immediately

- Eliminate neatness as grading criteria, except on computer-generated papers.

- Decrease copying aspects of assignments lie offering a math workbook instead of needing student to copy issues from the book. A copying buddy can assist in copying the issues with the use of a carbon paper.

- Let and encourage use of abbreviation for in-class writing assignments like b/4 for before. Have the student get a list of appropriate abbreviation in his workbook and taped to his desk for simple reference. Start with some and increase as the first few become automatic.

- Have students who are much younger use large graph paper for math calculation to keep columns and rows straight. Older student may use loose leaf paper changed sideways to aid maintain straight columns.

- Reinforce the positive aspects of student's efforts.

- Also encourage student to be patient.

Creativity note

Dysgraphia doesn't have to reduce creativity, as seen by the sample below composed by a twelve year old dysgraphic and dyslexic student.

1.   Exact story: student read to teacher making use of his draft;

The way I describe a bumpy ride is similar to a Wolfgang Mozart's music. Every bumpy road is just like a song. Every bump on the way is a note. Every bump is not controlled at the exact time it still is controlled. That was the magic to Mozart's music. It was not understandable and predictable. Therefore, the next time you drive down a bumpy road, have thoughts on Mozart.

2.   First draft of creative story typed by a twelve year old student

The way I describe a bumpy ride is similar to wothgan mowsarts moweek. Eshe bumpy rowd is like a song. Eshe bump is the note eche uncon at the exact time ste is. That was the mewstere to mowths it was vare meterus and unperdedable. Therefore, the next time you drive diwn a bumoy theak of mowsart.

A Note with regards to development of word processing skills

Various dysgraphic students find it tough with correct fingering in keyboarding skills. Nevertheless,, it is critical to expose students to the correct fingering to grow quick visual locating skills for letters on the keyboard, perfectly without having to look every time. One critical strategy is to possess the student practice keyboarding skills close to ten times every day.

The student should use various child-oriented typing tutor programs and work to grow appropriate skills to increase her ability. Also, whenever the student types for content or ideas, whether a sentence, word, or an entire paragraph, she should be permitted to use whatever fingering she desires.

At the end, the objective is for the student to automatically incorporate at least a few correct keyboards fingering when typing content.

Chapter Six

Treating Dysgraphia with Therapy

Either your child or you can benefit from an occupational therapist, especially if you find it difficult with the fine motor skills that have do with writing. The occupational therapy is majorly used in treating children that suffer from dysgraphia. However, few occupational therapists work with grown-ups, as well.

Occupational therapy may include controlling different materials to create wrist and hand strength, practicing cursive writing, running letter formation drills, which is simpler than writing. Easy repetitive movements such as taking pegs out of a pegboard and placing them back in, can assist an individual with dysgraphia have finger strength that will enable your writing to be much more spontaneous and easier.

Grown-ups or adults that suffer from dysgraphia who went through childhood without suffering from dysgraphia might have unresolved feelings of anger and shame connecting to the condition and will gain from communicating with a psychotherapist to discuss some difficult emotions. In spite of one's age, it is vital for people that are suffering from dysgraphia to acknowledge that suffering from dysgraphia is nothing to feel embarrassed of as psychotherapy can be advantageous for solving the problem of building self-esteem and anger.

Remedy for Dysgraphia

To bring an end to a child's dysgraphia, ensure that after close attention to the above stated symptoms, the child should relate to any. Remedying this impairment will be of great help to the child as he will not get to grow to face difficulties while writing. Here is what can be done to assist a child with dysgraphia to develop good writing skills.

Handwriting Activities

It will be difficult for the child to keep up with peer during class lectures or dictations. Both the class teacher and parents have a role to play as both would be helping the child by indulging him in writing exercises. This will help to bring about lettering interest from the child as well as groom the child cognitively to become sound in writing. Engage the child by mostly dictating texts and setting time-target for the child to reach. As time goes on, decrease the interval to see whether the child will still level up.

Adjust to Contain the Child

Concluding that such a child is unintelligent will only lead to the child becoming unintelligent. With this impairment corrected, the child will become very functional even in other learning skills. Where the child gets it wrong, encourage and provide him extra activities to bolster his learning.

Expose the Child to the Word Processing Applications

This will help the child to learn beyond just writing. Since one of the child's problems is memorization of language symbols, exposing the child to the use of these software allows him the room to learn and mastermind himself with the appearance of each lettered symbol.

How is dysgraphia analysed?

Diagnosing dysgraphia frequently requires a group of specialists, including a doctor and an authorized analyst or other emotional wellness proficient prepared in working with Children who have learning incapacities. A word related advisor, school analyst, or a specialized curriculum instructor may likewise help make the analysis.

For kids, some portion of the symptomatic procedure may incorporate an IQ test and an evaluation of their scholarly work. Explicit school assignments may likewise be inspected.

For grown-ups, instances of composed work or composed tests regulated by a specialist might be assessed. You will be seen as you write to search for fine engine aptitudes issues. You might be approached to duplicate words starting with one source then onto the next to help comprehend if there are language-preparing issues.

What medications are accessible?

Word related treatment might be useful in improving handwriting abilities. Remedial exercises may include:

- Holding a pencil or pen in another manner to make writing simpler

- Working with demonstrating earth
- Following letters in shaving cream on a work area
- Drawing lines inside labyrinths
- Doing draw an obvious conclusion confuses

There are likewise a few writing programs that can support kids and grown-ups structure letters and sentences conveniently on paper.

On the off chance that other learning inabilities or medical problems are available, treatment choices should address those conditions too. Meds might be expected to treat ADHD, for instance.

Chapter Seven

What to Do If Your Child Has Dysgraphia

Treatment

There's no solution for dysgraphia. Treatment shifts from child to child and relies upon whether he has some other learning incapacities or wellbeing conditions. Medication used to treat ADHD has assisted with dysgraphia in certain children who have the two conditions.

How Might I Help My Child?

Here are a few things you can attempt:

Have your child utilize wide-administered paper, chart paper, or paper with raised lines to help with letter and word arrangement.

Attempt pencil holds or other writing helps for comfort.

Let her utilization a PC to type rather than write, and show composing aptitudes early.

Try not to condemn messy work. Applause her difficult work and offer uplifting feedback.

Recognize the condition and converse with your child about it.

Show her approaches to mitigate worry before writing. For instance, have her shake or rub her hands together rapidly.

Let her crush a pressure ball to improve hand-muscle quality and coordination.

Converse with your child's instructor about her condition and needs at school. She may meet all requirements for a specialized curriculum administrations and an Individualized Education Program (IEP) or other uncommon help, (for example, a 504 arrangement). These reports detail your child's needs and give the school approaches to support her.

A few things you may request include:

- Shorter writing assignments or various inquiries from her cohorts
- Utilization of a PC to type rather than write
- Duplicates of the class notes to constrain writing work
- Utilization of a voice-to-transcription machine or another electronic note taker
- A choice to record the instructor's talks
- Video or sound reports rather than composed schoolwork assignments
- Oral rather than composed tests

Chapter Eight

Living with dysgraphia for Kids

For certain Children, word related treatment and engine aptitudes preparing can help improve their writing capacity. For other people, it stays a long lasting test.

In the event that you have a child or girl with dysgraphia, it's imperative to work with your kid's school and educators on housing that are suitable for this kind of learning incapacity. Some study hall techniques that may help include:

- An assigned note taker in the classroom
- Utilization of a PC for notes and different assignments
- Oral tests and assignments, rather than composed ones
- Additional time on tests and assignments
- Exercise or talk notes gave by the instructor as printouts, chronicles, or in advanced structure

- Pencils or other writing executes with exceptional grasps to make writing simpler
- Utilization of wide-managed or chart paper

What's more, on the off chance that you feel that the treatment you or youngsters get for dysgraphia isn't adequate, don't surrender. Search for different specialists or assets in your locale that may help. You may should be a forceful supporter for your youngster, yet remember that there are laws and school arrangements intended to serve understudies with a wide range of learning difficulties.

Chapter Nine

Fun Activities to Correct Dysgraphia in Children

If your child has Dysgraphia – which we already know is a learning disability that causes symptoms like writing difficulties or illegible handwriting that can also include inappropriate pencil nip or inconsistent pencil grip, then there are activities that can help solve this disability.

Dysgraphia can lead to reading and spelling difficulties if nothing is done on time to correct it. There are several activities that can help a child with dysgraphia. A lot of kids have also benefitted from several modified assignments that lessen the need for them to write.

Some of the activities that can help your child overcome Dysgraphia includes;

Forming Letters

A child with Dysgraphia must know how to form letters properly. Some early activities to help them include;

- Tracing letters with a pointer tool or their fingers

- Connecting dots to form a letter

- Copying specific model letters and then following instruction on a step-by-step letter formation

Paper Mazes

Putting pencil/pen to paper requires great motor control. That skill can be learnt via puzzles like paper mazes. To reach the end of the maze, your kid must steady their writing material within the strict boundary, which helps to improve their coordination.

Motor Control

A child with dysgraphia might find it difficult with fine motor skills and ability to control muscles. It is advisable to give them a modeling dough or clay to knead, it helps them build stronger hand muscles.

Paper mazes on the other hand allow the child the opportunity to practice a fine motor control and develop their hand muscles. They thread the maze using a pencil line. This offers them the opportunity to work on their muscles without the need of creating a legible handwriting.

Dexterity and finger strength plays a crucial role in a child's handwriting. If you child has dysgraphia as a kid, encourage them to play with clay for 35 minutes a day. The clay will help strengthen their hand muscles and help them improve the way they control writing materials.

Letter Writing

Children with dysgraphia who know how to form letters improve more from activities that involves handwriting practice and letter formation according to the international dyslexia association.

Letter writing provide children the chance to create letter from their memory and the opportunity to write dictated letters with or without any external help of a step-by-step writing guide. It also offers students a wider range of writing materials and papers to help make their letter writing fun.

Handwriting

It is also important to help the child with several handwriting activities which also includes showing the child how to use cursive writing since many students with dysgraphia find cursive simpler to write according the Reading Rocket organization.

Other activities that can help a child with dysgraphia includes giving the child a short period to write on anything they feel like writing. Also, a parent or teacher can focus on dictation and handwriting. It helps children with dysgraphia learn letter formation and handwriting skills.

Writing Stages

For older children with dysgraphia, their activities should focus on instruction on writing a research or composition. Teach the child how to break down writing into several stages to avoid getting overwhelmed.

Composition can be broken into stages such as draft writing, rewriting, brainstorming, editing, proofreading, outlining and allow the children work on each of the step individually. You can also teach your child simple marks and abbreviations used in editing, to reduce the number of writing necessary.

At school, you can tell the teacher to allow your child take part in peer writing reviews and spell checking. This is to help them see their writing from another child's perspective and gain valuable insight into how to find words that have been misspelt.

Memory Games

Dysgraphia disorder causes impairment of orthographic coding. It causes problems to the process of storing new words in the working memory, while analyzing each letter. To help your child overcome this problem and improve their handwriting skill, try saying words aloud and instruct them to visualize it. Few seconds later, have them write the words they've memorized on any piece of paper.

Prompts

Once your child becomes comfortable with writing and memorizing individual letters, you can comfortably move them into full words and sentences. You can introduce it to them by giving them an amusing prompt and allowing them five minutes to compose a small related text.

Dictation

For a child with dysgraphia, dictation is a fun way to improve your child's orthographic coding abilities and handwriting. You can read a letter aloud and have your child copy it down. To make it more fun, try selecting a series of letter that spell out funny words that the child is familiar with.

A lot of children have dysgraphia and it currently affects thousands of kids nationwide. It significantly impairs one's handwriting and their ability to confidently express themselves via written language.

As a parent, these steps listed above can help you inspire confidence in your child and help them. Not only their handwriting, but their confidence.

Made in the USA
Middletown, DE
23 September 2023